The Anansi Tales

An Ashanti Story From Africa

Retold by Helen Bethune
Illustrated by Lorraine Hannay

CELEBRATION PRESS
Pearson Learning Group

A long, long time ago, there were no stories to tell.

Nyame, the Sky God, had come down to Earth and had stolen all the stories.

He had placed them all in a beautiful treasure box, and hidden the box under his throne.

Anansi was a young man who wanted all the stories back. He wanted children to be able to listen to stories.

He decided speak with Nyame to see if he could afford to buy the stories from him.

He spun a magic web and climbed up to the heavens. He arrived right at the entrance of Nyame's palace.

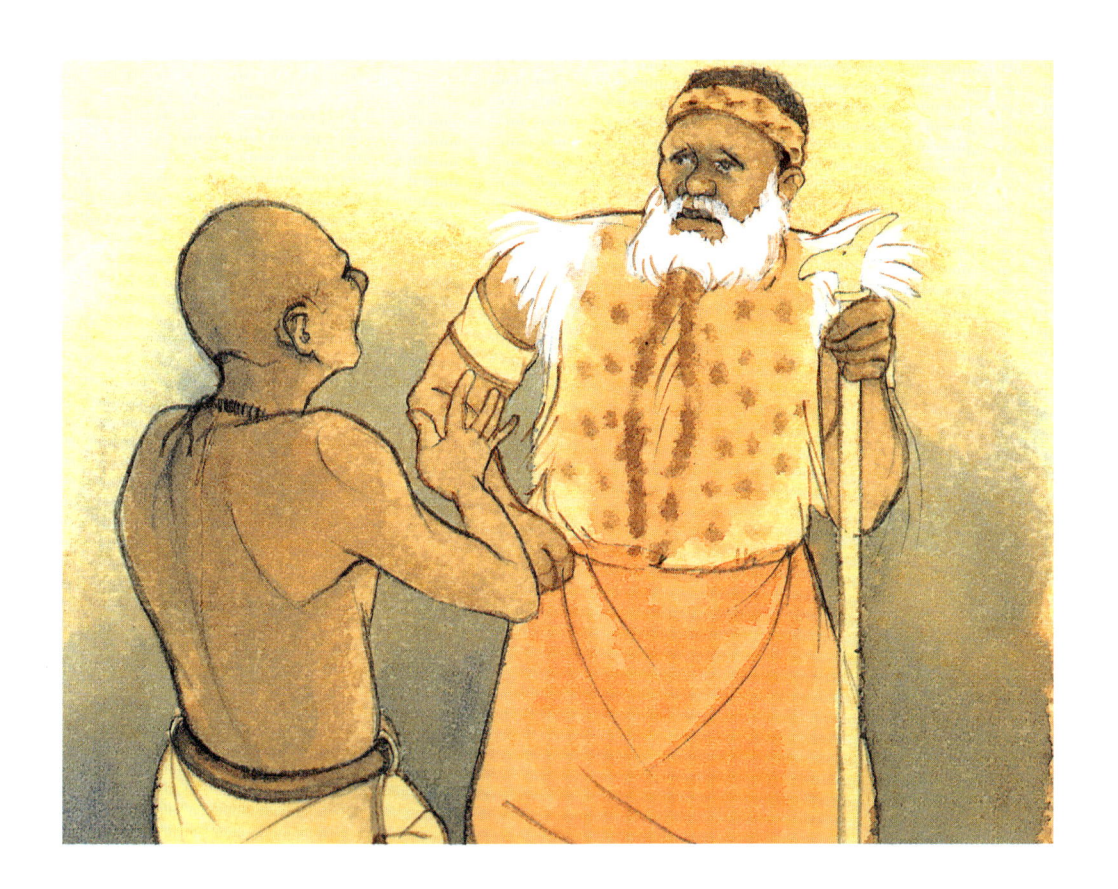

Boldly, he said to Nyame, "You must return the stories. The people on Earth are very unhappy for the children, who have nothing to listen to. They want to hear about their culture."

"I can return the stories," Nyame said, "but the price will be very, very high."

Anansi knew that no price would be too high to make the children on Earth happy.

"I'll do anything," he said.

"First, I want you to bring me three hairs from a ferocious lion," Nyame said.

Anansi nodded.

"Second, there's an old crocodile down at the river. I want you to bring me up one of his teeth," Nyame continued.

Anansi nodded again.

"Third, I want you to bring to me a special little fairy, called Mmoatia, that no one has ever seen. He comes just before dawn, and he leaves before it is light."

Anansi nodded for the third time.

"I'll be back in a few days," he said.

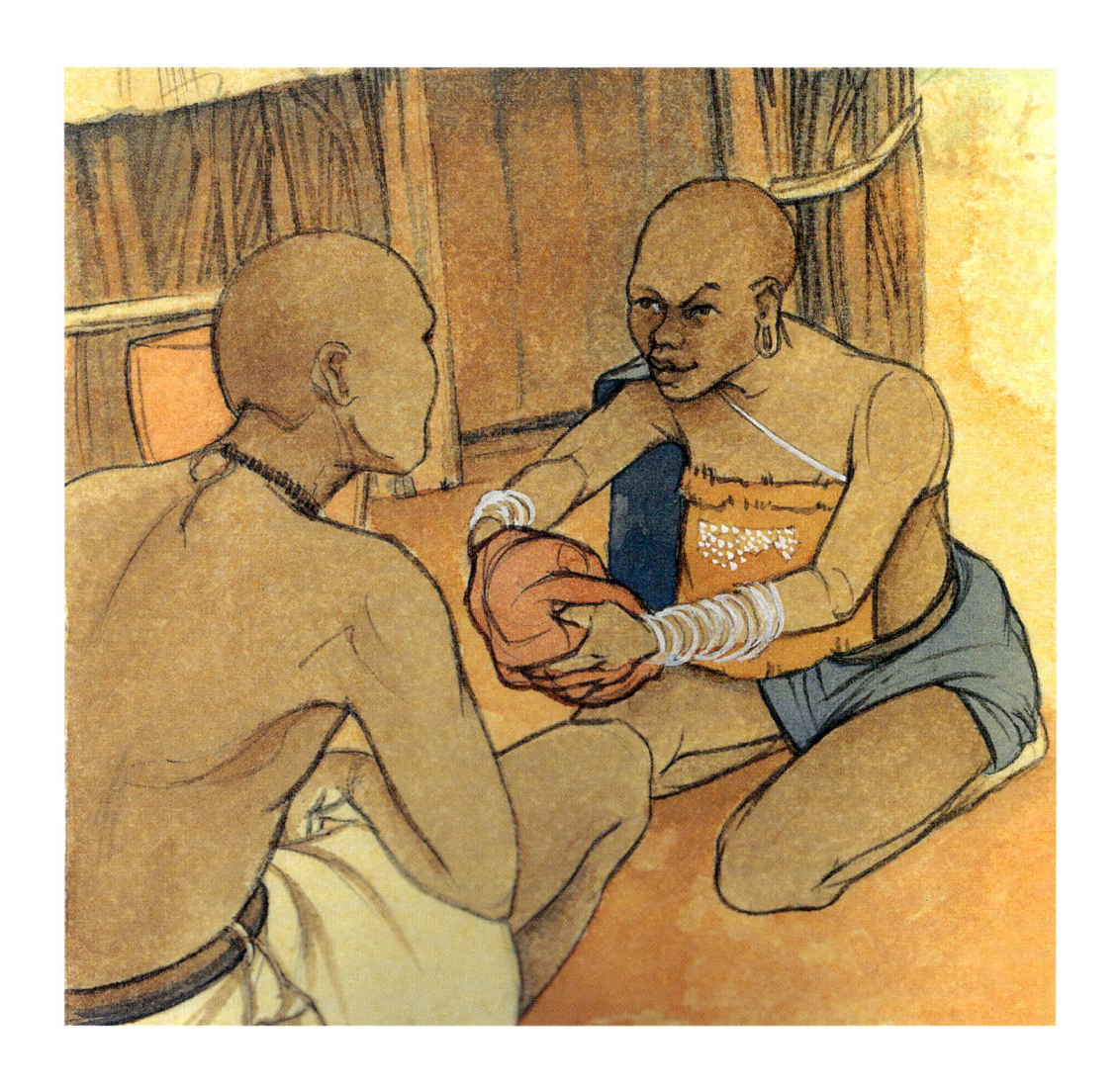

Anansi climbed back down his web and went home. He told his wife, Aso, about what he had said he would do.

Aso said, "I've seen that lion down at the water hole. I'm sure he comes around 12 o'clock. If you go there then, you can get him. Take this meat with you."

So Anansi went down to the water hole. Sure enough, the lion came straight for the water.

Anansi tried to creep close to the lion. He was very scared.

He crept closer to the lion, and he was even more scared.

He held the meat out in front of him and the lion looked up and smelled it.

He came very close until the lion was eating the meat from Anansi's hand.

As the lion ate the meat, Anansi stroked his mane. And as he stroked his mane he pulled out three beautiful hairs—pop, pop, pop.

He dropped the rest of the meat and ran away.

As he ran, he wrapped up the three hairs in a banana leaf and put them in his pouch.

He thought to himself proudly, "That's one of my tasks done! But how do I find that old crocodile? How do I get him up from the bottom of that water?"

He went home again to ask Aso for advice.

She told him, "Take this stick, and go to the river. If you beat the water long enough, the crocodile will come up."

Anansi thought to himself, "Why didn't I think of that?"

He grabbed the stick, went down to the river, and he beat the water. He pounded the water!

Water went up and down, the fish came up and down, and down and around!

The old crocodile wondered what was going on. He came up to the surface!

There he saw Anansi beating and beating the water with the stick.

The old crocodile came up and opened his big mouth, but before he could ask, "What are you doing?" Anansi stuck the stick in the crocodile's mouth.

He jammed the old crocodile's mouth wide open.

Then he reached right into his gaping jaws and pulled out a huge old tooth.

As he washed the tooth and wrapped it up, Anansi said, "A job well done. Two of my tasks are now complete!"

He went back home to talk to Aso again. He asked her, "How can I find this fairy that no one has ever seen? What can I do?"

Aso answered, "If he only appears between the night and the morning, you must go to the forest and sleep by an old tree. But first, you must smear your body with the sap of the tree. And then pretend to be asleep."

Anansi started to set off.

"But don't fall asleep!" Aso warned. "You might miss him."

So Anansi did what Aso said. He smeared his body with sap, and then he sat beside the oldest tree in the forest.

Soon night came.

Anansi fell asleep!

Luckily, he woke up just before dawn.

He saw Mmoatia, the little fairy. He had arrived just as the dew was falling from the trees.

Mmoatia swirled around and around. As he came near the tree, he saw Anansi.

Anansi quickly closed his eyes and didn't move a muscle.

Mmoatia moved closer to Anansi, and then closer still.

Then he reached out and touched Anansi.

His hand was stuck!

"Let go of my hand," he cried. "Let go of my hand!"

He put his other hand there to try to release the first, but it stuck too.

"Let go of my hand!" he cried.

Then he put one foot up, and tried to pull his hands away.

Now his foot was stuck.

The fairy could now only hop!

He was very angry!

Anansi opened his eyes and smiled and said, "I've got you."

He unstuck Mmoatia and put him inside his pouch.

"Another job well done!" he said.

Now Anansi had everything he needed to take to Nyame.

Anansi climbed his web again and arrived at Nyame's palace in the sky.

"Nyame, I have brought you everything you asked for."

Nyame wanted to see for himself.

"First, let me see the hairs from the lion," he said.

Anansi pulled the three beautiful lion hairs from one of his pouches.

Nyame was happy.

"But what about the crocodile's tooth?" he demanded.

Anansi pulled the tooth out of another pouch.

Nyame was delighted!

Then Nyame cried, "But best of all, where is Mmoatia? I must have that little fairy that no one has seen!"

Anansi pulled out the teeny little fairy. He was very sticky. (And very angry!)

Anansi cleaned him as best he could, but Nyame was still happy. (Mmoatia was still very angry!)

"Anansi, you have done what no other has done before. I have what I want, and now I shall give you what you want."

Reaching under his throne, he brought out the treasure chest and gave it to Anansi.

"Thank you," said Anansi. "Now I can make all the children in the world happy."

As Anansi climbed back down to Earth, he opened the treasure chest wide. Stories began to fly to all corners of the world. Every which way they went, flying here, floating there, going back to where they belonged.

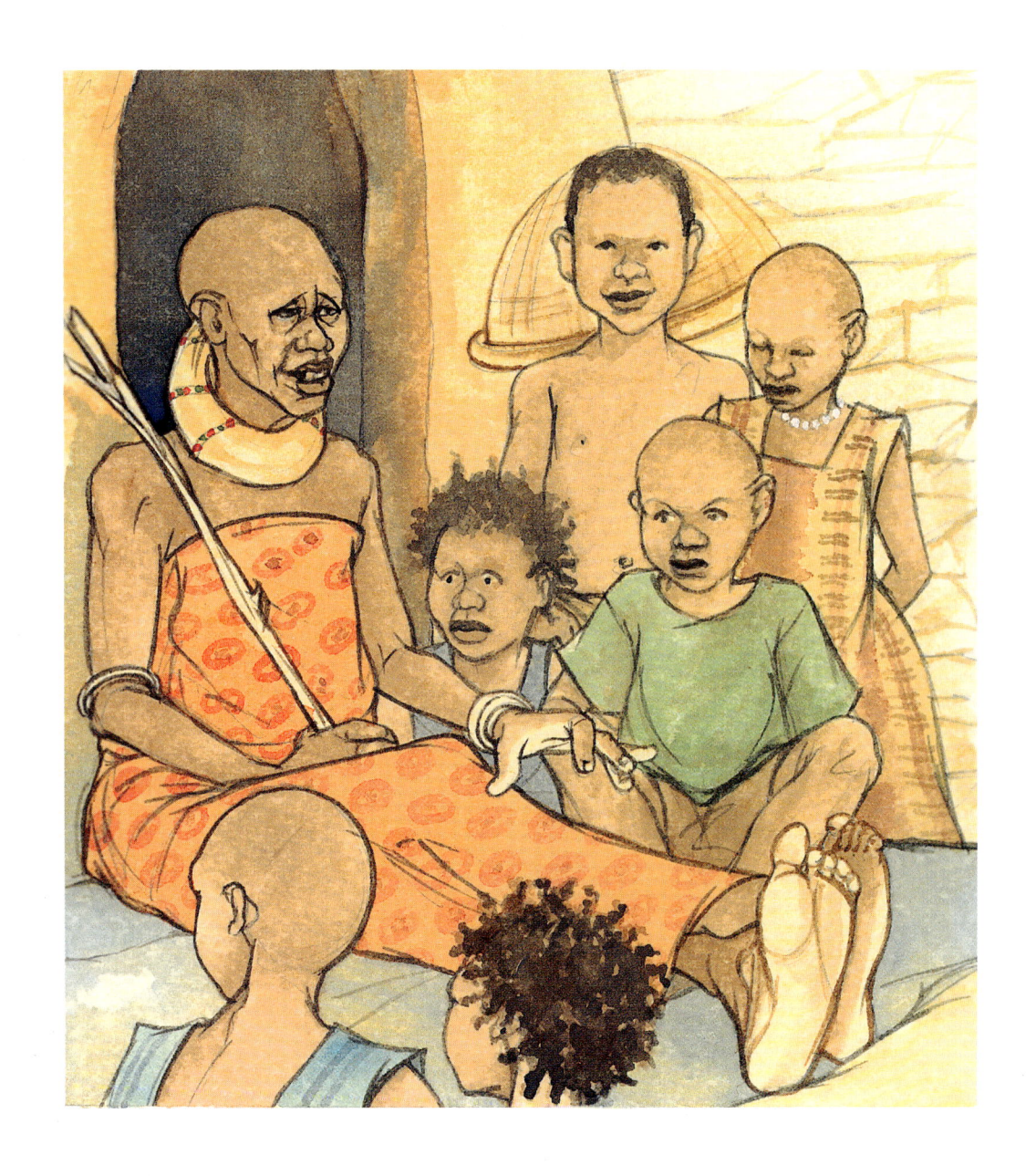

And that is how Anansi returned all the stories to the people of the world.

They are called the Anansi Tales.